SHARKS

Q2AMedia

Created by Q2AMedia
www.q2amedia.com
Text, design & illustrations copyright © 2009 Q2AMedia

Editor Honor Head
Publishing Director Chester Fisher
Creative Director Simmi Sikka
Senior Designers Rahul Dhiman and Joita Das

Client Service Manager Ravneet Kaur
Project Manager Shekhar Kapur
Illustrators Subhash Vohra, Aadil A. Siddiqui and Amit Tayal
Art Editor Sujatha Menon
Picture Researcher Lalit Dalal

Tangerine Press edition copyright © 2009 Scholastic Inc.

an imprint of
SCHOLASTIC
www.scholastic.com

Scholastic and Tangerine Press and associated logos are trademarks of Scholastic Inc.

Published by Tangerine Press, an imprint of Scholastic Inc.,
557 Broadway, New York, NY 10012

Scholastic New Zealand Ltd.
Greenmount, Auckland

Scholastic Canada Ltd.
Markham, Ontario

Scholastic Australia Pty. Ltd
Gosford NSW

Scholastic UK
Coventry, Warwickshire

10 9 8 7 6 5 4 3 2 1

ISBN-10: 0-545-08485-7
ISBN-13: 978-0-545-08485-7

Printed in China

About The Author

A biologist with a passion for the sea and its inhabitants, Stephen Savage also spends a lot of his time preparing school workshops on the oceans to help create a respect and understanding of our seas in children of all ages. He lives in the UK and is involved in a local study of sea mammals and assists in a sea mammal rescue program.

Picture Credits
t=top, tr=top right, tl=top left, bl= bottom left, br=bottom right, b=bottom

Cover Images:
Front: Q2AMedia Artwork.

Back: Brian J. Skerry/National Geographic/ Getty Images.

Full Title: Ian Scott: Shutterstock.
Imprint: Stephen Sweet: Shutterstock.
Half Title: Peter Arnold, Inc.: Alamy.
Content images: tr cbpix: Shutterstock.

bl SeaPics.com. br Aleksandrs Marinicevs: Shutterstock.

6-7m Doug Perrine: Naturepl. **6-7b** Stasys Eidiejus: Shutterstock. **8bl** Seapics.com.
12 SeaPics.com. **14** SeaPics.com. **15t** SeaPics.com. **15br** SeaPics.com. **16-17b** SeaPics.com. **16t** SeaPics.com. **18** Doug Perrine: Naturepl. **19b** SeaPics.com. **21** Marinethemes. **22** SeaPics.com. **23t** SeaPics.com. **23b** Aleksandrs Marinicevs: Shutterstock. **24t** SeaPics.com. **24b** SeaPics.com. **26** SeaPics.com. **27tr** Stephen Frink Collection: Alamy. **27br** Carl Roessler: Pacific Stock: Photolibrary. **28** SeaPics.com.

30 SeaPics.com. **30ml** SeaPics.com. **32** Jeff Rotman: Naturepl. **34-35** Danita Delimont: Alamy. **35tr** Brent Hedges: Naturepl. **36** SeaPics.com. **37** SeaPics.com **38** Chris and Monique Fallows: Oxford Scientific (OSF): Photolibrary. **40** Colin Speedie **41** Jeff Rotman: Alamy. **42-43** Jeff Rotman: Naturepl. **43tr** Georgette Douwma: Naturepl. **43br** Jurgen Freund: Naturepl.
44 Ian Scott: Shutterstock. **45tr** Jurie Maree: Dreamstime. **45b** Harald Bolten: Dreamstime. **48** Dennis Sabo photography: Istockphoto.

Illustration: Q2AMedia ArtWork.

Face to Face

SHARKS

Stephen Savage

tangerine Press

an imprint of

SCHOLASTIC

www.scholastic.com

Contents

Helicoprion shark

crested horn shark

bull shark

thresher shark

GREENLAND

NORTH
AMERICA

*Atlantic
Ocean*

SOUTH
AMERICA

*Pacific
Ocean*

What Are Sharks?

Sharks are a type of fish found in nearly all the oceans of the world. Sharks swam in the sea long before dinosaurs roamed the Earth.

Seas full of sharks

There are 465 different species of shark. Some, such as the pygmy shark, are no bigger than a hand, while the whale shark can grow up to 40 ft. (12 m) long and weigh 20 tons (18 tonnes). Many sharks are powerful, streamlined hunters that cruise the oceans for food, but others, such as the horn shark, are small and live near the sea bed.

Unlike other fish, sharks, such as this Caribbean reef shark, do not have a bony skeleton but one made of tough, rubbery cartilage, which is lighter and more flexible than bone.

EUROPE

ASIA

AFRICA

Pacific Ocean

ntic
n

Indian Ocean

AUSTRALIA

Most sharks live in the seas, but some, such
as the bull shark, can live in freshwater rivers
and lakes for long periods of time. This map
shows the main areas of the world where some
shark species can be found.

Great white shark

Mako shark

Hammerhead shark

Whale shark

Grey nurse shark

Whitetip reef shark

Basking shark

Prehistoric Sharks

Sharks have lived in the oceans for millions of years. In prehistoric times, the oceans were filled with strange-looking sharks.

Scary ancestors

Ancient sharks came in many shapes and sizes. There is fossil evidence for more than 3,000 different kinds of prehistoric sharks. The *Hybodus* was the most common type of shark during the age of the dinosaurs, and some scientists believe it is the ancestor of some modern sharks.

Dorsal fin spine may have stopped other sharks from trying to swallow it.

Teeth talk

Sharks shed their teeth as they grow, so there are many fossilized shark teeth. Most of what we know comes from a few complete fossils and mainly fossilized teeth and skin.

◄ *This is a fossil tooth of the extinct* Carcharodon megalodon, *which looked like the great white shark but grew to twice the size.*

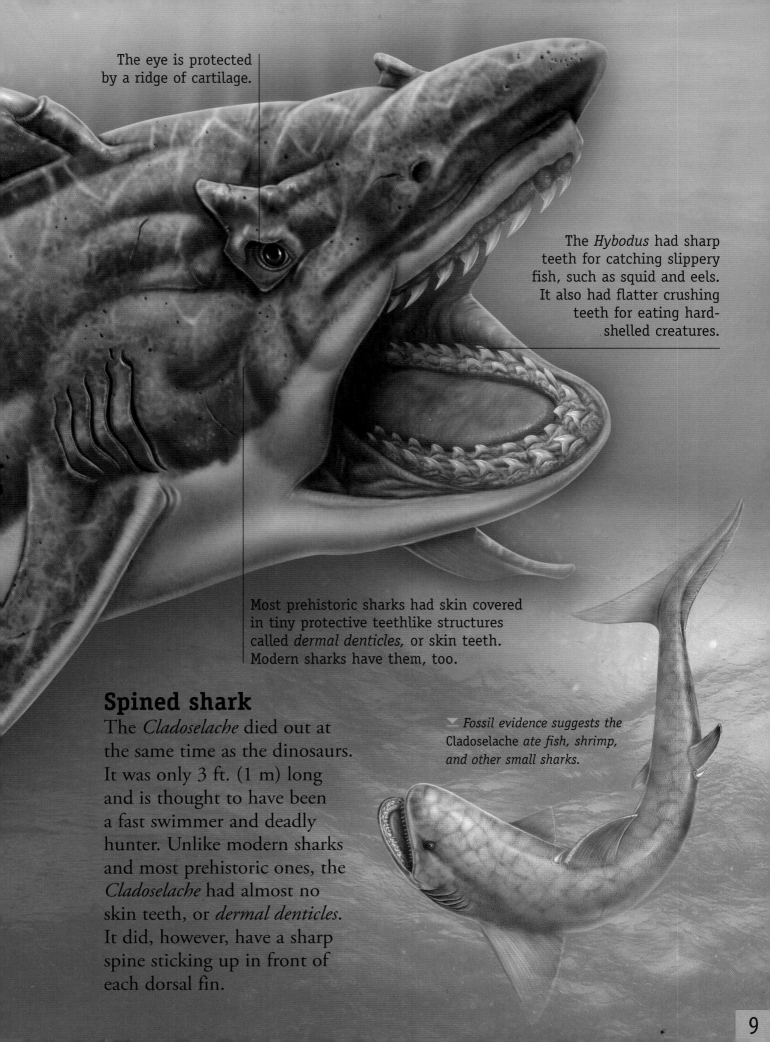

The eye is protected by a ridge of cartilage.

The *Hybodus* had sharp teeth for catching slippery fish, such as squid and eels. It also had flatter crushing teeth for eating hard-shelled creatures.

Most prehistoric sharks had skin covered in tiny protective teethlike structures called *dermal denticles,* or skin teeth. Modern sharks have them, too.

Spined shark

The *Cladoselache* died out at the same time as the dinosaurs. It was only 3 ft. (1 m) long and is thought to have been a fast swimmer and deadly hunter. Unlike modern sharks and most prehistoric ones, the *Cladoselache* had almost no skin teeth, or *dermal denticles.* It did, however, have a sharp spine sticking up in front of each dorsal fin.

▼ *Fossil evidence suggests the* Cladoselache *ate fish, shrimp, and other small sharks.*

Pretend teeth

The *Stethacanthus* was a very peculiar shark. It had a flattened dorsal fin on its back covered in extra-large, teethlike scales that looked like a brush. It also had a similar patch on top of its head. Scientists believe that these patches could have looked like an open jaw meant to frighten off predators attacking it from above.

▲ *The patch of teeth on the* Stethacanthus's *head could have been used in head-to-head pushing contests with other males at mating time.*

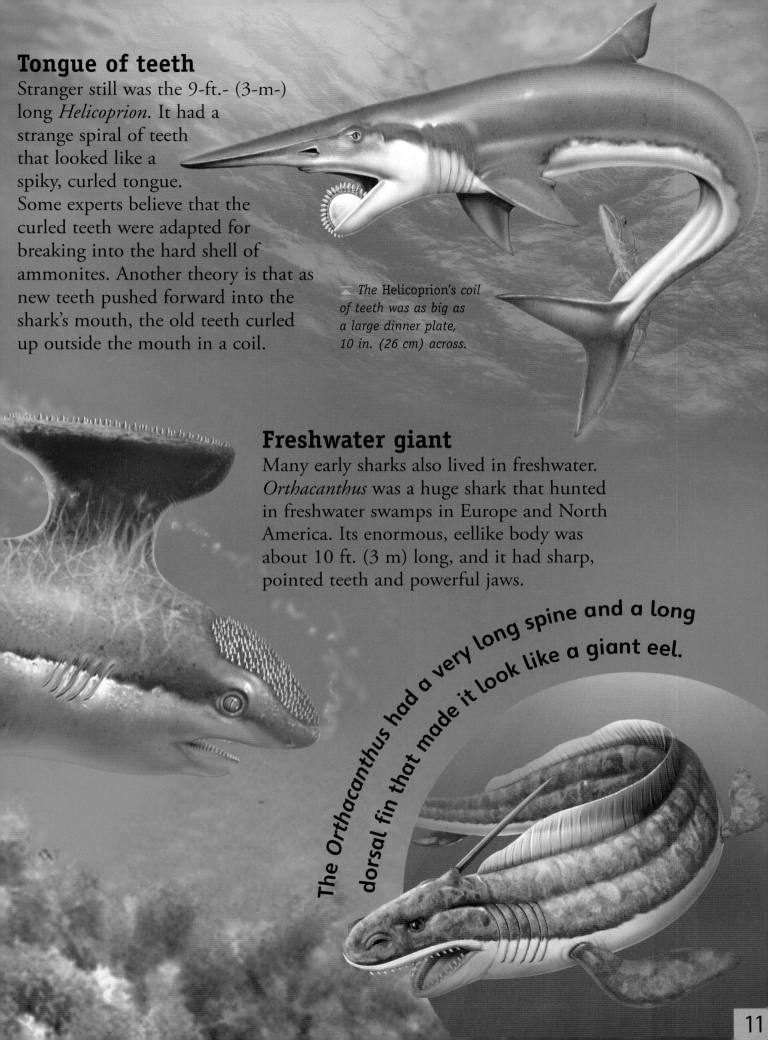

Tongue of teeth

Stranger still was the 9-ft.- (3-m-) long *Helicoprion*. It had a strange spiral of teeth that looked like a spiky, curled tongue. Some experts believe that the curled teeth were adapted for breaking into the hard shell of ammonites. Another theory is that as new teeth pushed forward into the shark's mouth, the old teeth curled up outside the mouth in a coil.

The Helicoprion's coil of teeth was as big as a large dinner plate, 10 in. (26 cm) across.

Freshwater giant

Many early sharks also lived in freshwater. *Orthacanthus* was a huge shark that hunted in freshwater swamps in Europe and North America. Its enormous, eellike body was about 10 ft. (3 m) long, and it had sharp, pointed teeth and powerful jaws.

The Orthacanthus had a very long spine and a long dorsal fin that made it look like a giant eel.

Shark Waters!

There are sharks in almost every sea of the world. They may live in the open ocean, along warm coastal waters, on the sandy seabed, or in the dark ocean depths.

Whale shark

Although at 40 ft. (12 m) long the whale shark is the largest of all sharks, it is a gentle giant. It lives in the warm, tropical waters of the Atlantic and the Pacific and often will swim on the surface. It has a huge, cavernous mouth, which it uses to catch small fish and *plankton*, which are tiny ocean creatures.

The whale shark is very curious and will allow divers to swim with it and sometimes even to hitch a ride.

Special spots

Each whale shark has a unique pattern of spots. This means that individual sharks can be easily recognized. Whale sharks will usually travel great distances, but divers have noticed that the same sharks often return to the same area each year.

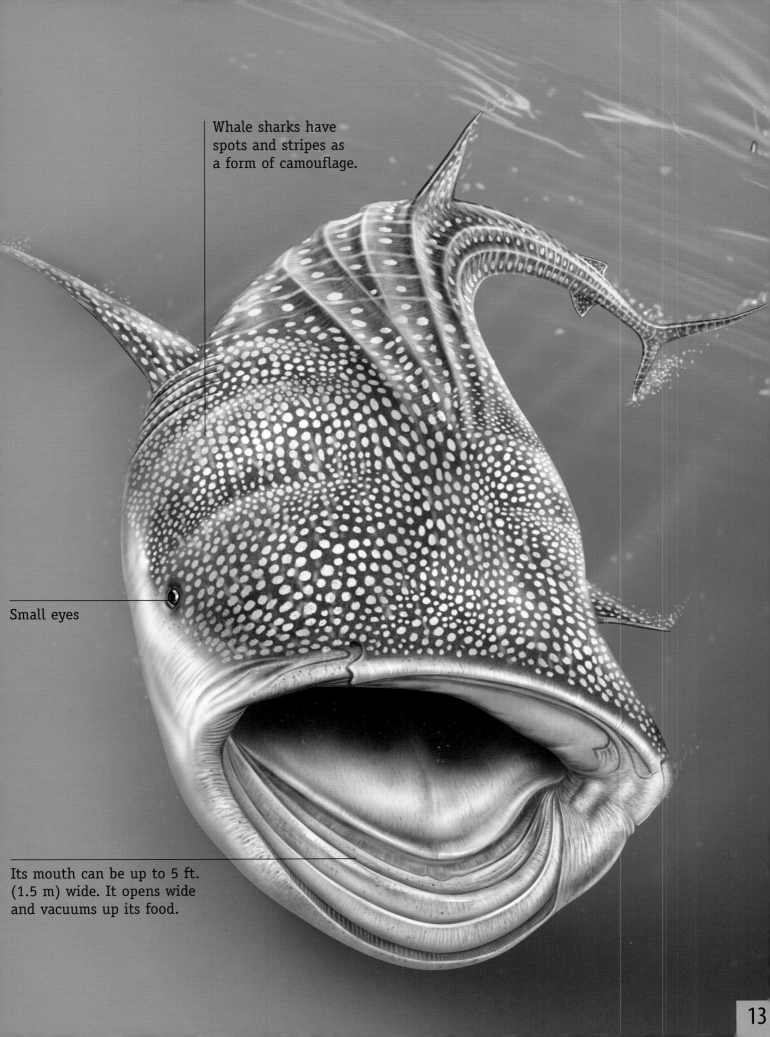

Whale sharks have spots and stripes as a form of camouflage.

Small eyes

Its mouth can be up to 5 ft. (1.5 m) wide. It opens wide and vacuums up its food.

The hammerhead

Scientists believe that its strange-shaped head may make the hammerhead's senses more effective. It is known that great hammerheads use the sides of their heads to pin a ray to the seabed before biting a chunk from its fins. The ray is then unable to escape, and the hammerhead continues to eat it. The great hammerhead shark is often found in tropical and subtropical waters of the Atlantic and the Pacific. It feeds on rays and a wide variety of fish, including small sharks.

The hammerhead's eyes and nostrils are at each end of its head.

FACT

The bull shark usually lives in saltwater but also has been seen in freshwater rivers, such as the Amazon River in South America, hundreds of miles away from the sea.

Whitetip reef shark

As its name suggests, this shark has a white tip on its fins. It likes warm, shallow, clear waters, such as coral reefs and bays. During the day groups of whitetip reef sharks like to rest in caves or tucked into cracks in the coral reefs. They will use the same cave for a long time before suddenly deciding to find somewhere else to rest.

▲ Whitetip reef sharks spend most of their time at the bottom of the ocean. They hunt at night, feeding on octopus, fish, and crabs.

Fast mover

Many species of shark live in the temperate waters between the tropical seas and the polar oceans. These species include the leopard shark, which lives at the sea bottom, and the basking shark and porbeagle shark, which live in the open waters. The porbeagle belongs to a group known as mackerel sharks, which also includes the great white shark.

▶ Leopard sharks live in rocky reefs and sandy areas along the Pacific coast of the U.S.

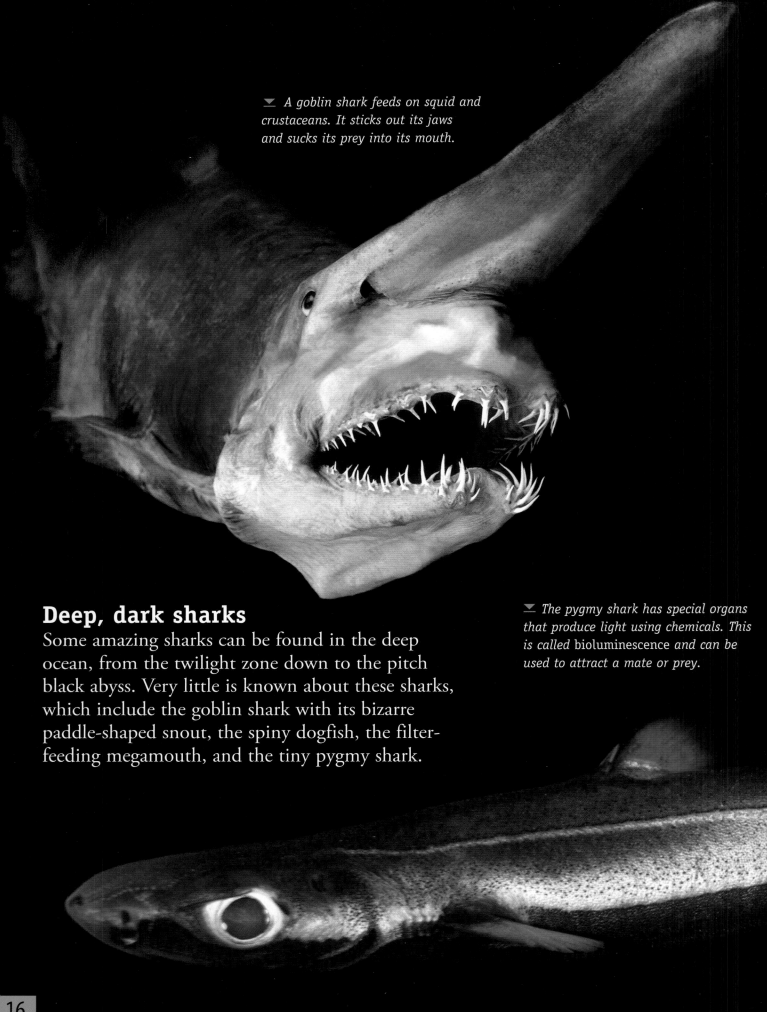

▼ A goblin shark feeds on squid and crustaceans. It sticks out its jaws and sucks its prey into its mouth.

Deep, dark sharks

Some amazing sharks can be found in the deep ocean, from the twilight zone down to the pitch black abyss. Very little is known about these sharks, which include the goblin shark with its bizarre paddle-shaped snout, the spiny dogfish, the filter-feeding megamouth, and the tiny pygmy shark.

▼ The pygmy shark has special organs that produce light using chemicals. This is called bioluminescence and can be used to attract a mate or prey.

Slow growers

Greenland sharks can be found deep in the icy polar waters of the Arctic Ocean. The Greenland shark can reach 21 ft. (6.5 m) long but grows slowly because of the cold water. Greenland sharks prey on a wide range of cold-water fish and also eat the dead remains of large sea creatures, such as whales. Even though they are slow moving, they are able to catch small sea mammals, such as seals.

⏶ Greenland sharks live at a depth of 1,800 ft. (550 m), much deeper than most other sharks.

FACT

Much of the deepest parts of the ocean are still unexplored. There may be shark species yet to be discovered.

The Search for Food

Some sharks are fearsome meat eaters and can hunt down prey over a wide area. Other sharks just open wide and take in a huge gulp of seawater and food.

Danger! Shark!

The great white shark is the ultimate ocean predator and the largest meat-eating fish. It eats a wide range of prey, including large tuna and elephant seals. Its teeth in the lower jaw hold the prey while the teeth in the upper jaw slice downward, removing large chunks that are then swallowed.

The great white shark's jaws are filled with large, serrated, triangular teeth.

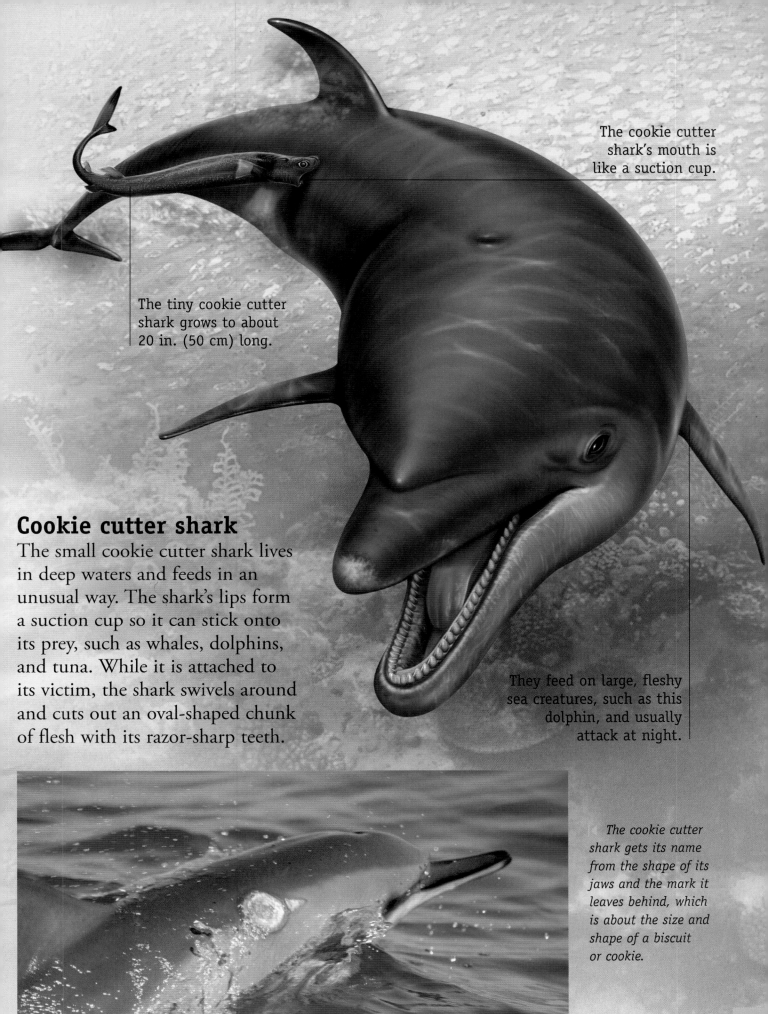

The cookie cutter shark's mouth is like a suction cup.

The tiny cookie cutter shark grows to about 20 in. (50 cm) long.

Cookie cutter shark

The small cookie cutter shark lives in deep waters and feeds in an unusual way. The shark's lips form a suction cup so it can stick onto its prey, such as whales, dolphins, and tuna. While it is attached to its victim, the shark swivels around and cuts out an oval-shaped chunk of flesh with its razor-sharp teeth.

They feed on large, fleshy sea creatures, such as this dolphin, and usually attack at night.

The cookie cutter shark gets its name from the shape of its jaws and the mark it leaves behind, which is about the size and shape of a biscuit or cookie.

What a mouthful!

Some sharks have a completely different way of feeding. Big sharks, such as the whale shark, basking shark, and megamouth, have huge, cavernous mouths, but their tiny teeth are no longer used for tearing or chewing food. They feed by swimming through the water with their mouths open and scooping up huge mouthfuls of seawater full of plankton.

▼ *Inside the basking shark's mouth, each gill is protected by gill rakers. These trap the plankton and make sure they go straight down the shark's throat.*

⏞ *The Port Jackson shark is a type of bullhead shark. It has powerful jaws, which are used to grasp and crush its prey.*

Water filters

Sharks such as the basking shark are called *filter feeders*. Before the water passes out over the gills, food items are filtered out. The basking shark, for example, has special gill rakers attached to the inside of the gills, which filter out large quantities of plankton as the sea water gushes out. These plankton are the shark's food. A basking shark can filter 2,000 tons (1,814 tonnes) of water an hour.

Ground feeders

There are many sharks that live on the ocean floor, and these sharks have developed special techniques for feeding. The Port Jackson shark lives on the sea floor. It hunts at night, looking for crabs, sea urchins, snails, and fish. It has two types of teeth. Its front teeth are pointed for grasping prey, and its back teeth are flat and used to crush and grind the shells of its prey.

FACT

Tiger sharks will eat almost anything, including birds and other sharks. They have even been found with shoes, car tires, and nails in their stomachs.

Air sharks
Great white sharks have one of the most spectacular techniques for catching prey. In a few places around the world, great whites have developed a rather un-sharklike way of catching fast-moving seals and sea lions. They attack from below with such speed that they leap out of the water with their prey seized firmly in their jaws. These sharks have been nicknamed "air sharks."

Great white sharks have been seen breaching, or leaping out of the water, to catch their prey.

Feeding frenzy

A shark's senses can pick up the tiniest scent in the water, so the strong smell of dead food that is used by divers to attract sharks can completely overwhelm them. The smell of food is everywhere, and the sharks not only bite the food but each other. Feeding frenzies also can be triggered when fish blood is tipped into the water by shark fishermen to deliberately attract sharks for them to catch.

Hunting in pairs

Thresher sharks use their incredibly long tails to herd fish together to make them easier to catch. Thresher sharks usually travel alone but will often hunt in pairs, slapping the water with their tails to frighten the fish into a packed *shoal* (a large group). The sharks then lunge through the shoal, snapping up as many fish as they can. They may also use their tails to hit and stun prey.

⌧ *Dead food or fish blood poured into the sea attracts sharks from all around and can drive them into a feeding frenzy.*

⌧ *A thresher shark's tail can be up to 50 percent as long as its body.*

Super Senses

When a shark attacks, it appears suddenly. The prey is taken by surprise, but the shark has been tracking it for some time with its super senses and waiting for the right opportunity to strike.

Sensitive hearing

A shark's ability to see is limited by the murkiness of the water and how far away things are from it. Sound travels farther than light underwater, so sharks use their hearing as well as sight to hunt down prey. A shark's hearing is particularly sensitive to deeper, low-frequency sounds. These sounds include the movement of fish, seals, and even human swimmers.

Sight and senses

Sight, hearing, smell, and taste are constantly providing the shark with information about its environment. A shark's eyes are adapted to its way of living and hunting. The blue shark cruises the open waters and has large eyes for spotting prey a long way off. The horn shark lives on the ocean floor and has smaller eyes, as it relies on its other senses to find prey in darker waters.

The blue shark's eyes are very sensitive to light.

Like most sharks, this horn shark's eyesight is at its best at dawn and dusk, when most species hunt.

Some large sharks, such as this lemon shark, have a special membrane that moves up to cover their eyes to protect them from their prey while they feed.

The openings to a shark's ears are on top of its head and cannot be seen.

Sharks can pick up the smell of a creature that may have moved hundreds of miles away.

There are taste buds behind the teeth that tell a shark whether something is good to eat or not.

Smell and scent

A shark's sense of smell is one of its most important for hunting. Sharks can detect even the tiniest scent left behind by a passing fish. They will follow the trail left by the scent until they track down the fish. The blood from an injured animal is easier to pick up, as the scent is much stronger.

⌐ *When the scent is very strong, large numbers of sharks will head for the same place.*

Feeling and touching

Some bottom-living sharks catch prey that is hidden on the seabed. These species have special feelers, called *barbels*, which are sensitive to touch. The shark feels the seabed with its barbels in search of prey. Like most other fish, sharks have another sense called the *lateral line*. This is a row of tiny pores along the shark's head and body that can pick up vibrations and the movements of other animals.

The sawshark uses its feelers to find food under the sand. The snout is used to stir up the seabed and for slashing its prey.

Bite and spit

Sharks have taste buds just behind their teeth. These tell the shark how good to eat an animal or object is. Great white sharks have a habit called "bite, spit, and wait." One bite is enough for the shark to know if the prey is worth the energy it will take to kill and eat it. This is why sharks often stop an attack after only one bite.

▶ Most sharks play an important role in keeping the seas clean by feeding on dead or dying creatures. Such food is strong smelling and easily found.

Danger! Sharks!

Sharks are one of the most feared animals on Earth. They glide silently through the water to grab their victim. Their huge jaws and razor-sharp teeth can slice a human almost in half.

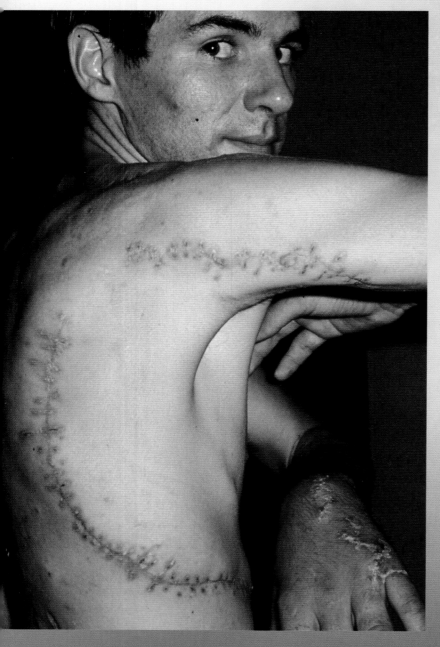

Shark attacks

A shark attack is fierce, but there is more danger in crossing a busy road or being struck by lightning than being injured by a shark. From all recorded attacks, three species stand out as being the most dangerous: the great white, tiger shark, and bull shark.

Great white shark

Experts believed that great white sharks attacked humans because they thought people were seals. But recent studies show a shark swims toward a surfer or swimmer slowly, carefully circling to see if the person is worth a closer look. Scientists now think that great whites take a chunk out of things they see in the water to "test" them to see if they are worth catching and eating.

Rodney Fox, South Australian spear-fishing champion, needed 462 stitches and many months to recover after an attack by a great white shark. Even so, he believes all sharks should be respected and protected. Rodney Fox went on to design and build the first observation shark cage.

Hitting its sensitive snout may drive away an attacking shark.

FACT

To help avoid being attacked by a shark, don't swim at dawn or dusk, don't swim if you're bleeding, and don't surf near seal colonies.

Garbage can of the seas

Tiger sharks are named for the striped markings they have when they are young, which fade as they get older. An adult may reach 13 ft. (4 m) in length. Unlike many other sharks, tiger sharks will eat anything, including fish, squid, seals, seabirds, sea turtles, and even garbage, such as old tin cans and beer bottles.

▲ A tiger shark's teeth are very distinctive. The teeth of the upper and lower jaw are the same shape, and are designed for cutting chunks from its prey.

On the prowl

Bull sharks can grow to up to 11 ft. (3.3 m) long and weigh 500 lbs. (226 kg). As a hunter in both salt and freshwater habitats, bull sharks feed on a wide variety of fish, birds, and sea mammals. They are aggressive hunters and prowl shallow waters looking for their next meal. However, like most sharks, they do not target humans—they are just searching for food and may mistake a human for normal prey.

▼ *Tiger sharks can be very dangerous because they are less fussy about what they eat. They like to eat large amounts of food and do not mind what the food tastes like.*

Right teeth for the job

Bull shark
Cutting teeth in the upper jaw with spiked, narrow teeth in the lower jaw.

Thresher shark
Teeth are curved and sharp, ideal for catching slippery fish and squid.

Tiger shark
Curved teeth with serrated edges and razor sharp for slicing through prey.

Mako shark
Long, thin, sharp teeth for catching slippery fish.

Great white shark
Triangular teeth with razor-sharp, serrated edges for cutting through flesh.

Nurse shark
Serrated, fan-shaped teeth for gripping fish and crushing shells.

FACT

Attacks by these kinds of sharks are very rare. Since 1876, tiger sharks have attacked 83 times with 29 fatalities, and bull sharks have attacked 69 times with 17 fatalities.

Survival!

Sharks have developed many survival techniques over the millions of years they have existed. One of the most amazing is their ability to constantly replace their teeth.

Never-ending teeth

Some sharks, such as the great white, have the most ferocious teeth of any living thing. Long and sharp, their teeth have serrated edges that can remove a chunk of flesh from the largest prey. Every time a large shark catches prey it loses a few teeth, but a great white shark can have up to 3,000 teeth during its lifetime. As old and damaged teeth fall out, new teeth from behind push forward and replace them.

Super jaws

Large, predatory sharks have jaws specially adapted for grasping or cutting prey. When the shark opens its mouth wide to snatch its prey, the upper jaw moves forward. With the help of powerful muscles, the shark can take a bite from even very large prey.

▼ *The teeth of great white sharks have a sharp point and serrated edges to help them grip and eat slippery prey.*

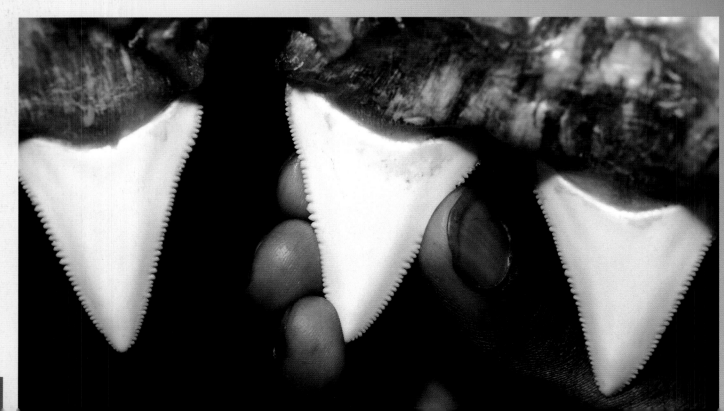

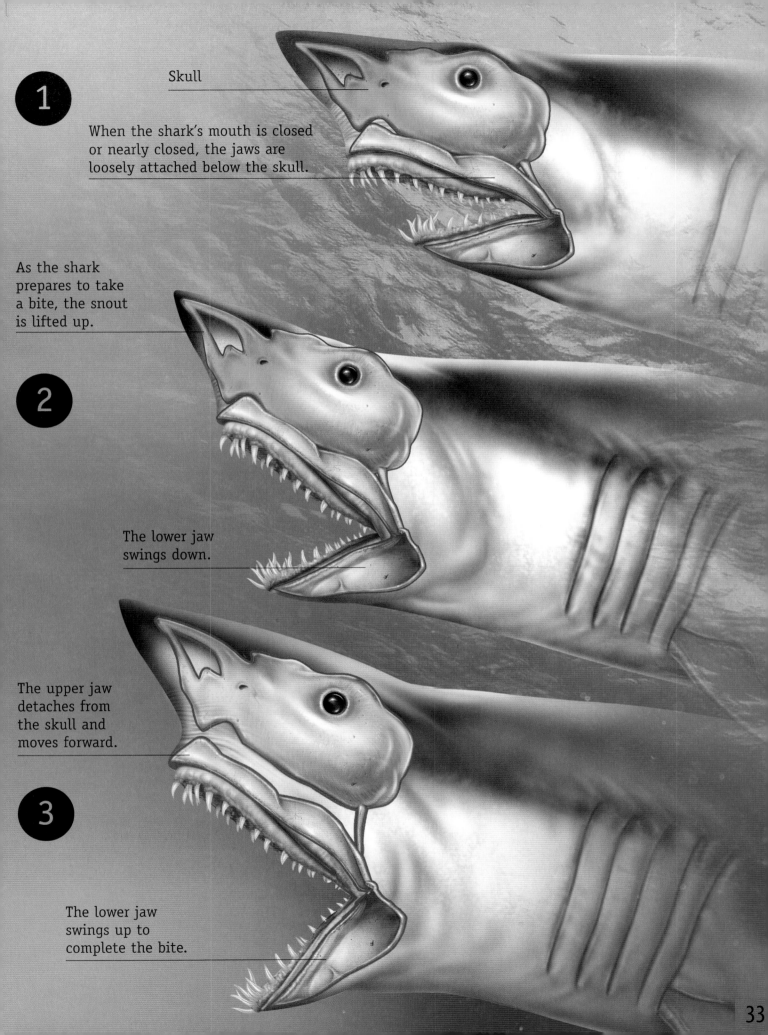

1

Skull

When the shark's mouth is closed or nearly closed, the jaws are loosely attached below the skull.

As the shark prepares to take a bite, the snout is lifted up.

2

The lower jaw swings down.

The upper jaw detaches from the skull and moves forward.

3

The lower jaw swings up to complete the bite.

Cunning camouflage

Many sharks are hunted by bigger sea creatures, so they need to protect themselves. Smaller sharks that live at the bottom of the ocean have skin that can be spotted, patchy, or striped. The pattern on their skin helps them to blend in with their surroundings. This is called *camouflage* and helps to hide them from enemies. Camouflage also can help sharks to catch unsuspecting prey that passes close by.

Wobbegong

Wobbegong sharks are also known as carpet sharks because they are flat and have mottled skin, which camouflages them against their surroundings. They rest on the seabed, on rocky ledges, and on coral reefs, waiting for prey to pass. When it does, they snatch it up with a snap of their jaws and swallow it whole. There are eight species, and each one has a different pattern depending on where it lives.

▶| *The tasselled wobbegong props itself up on its pectoral fins and attracts prey by wiggling the flaps of skin around its mouth.*

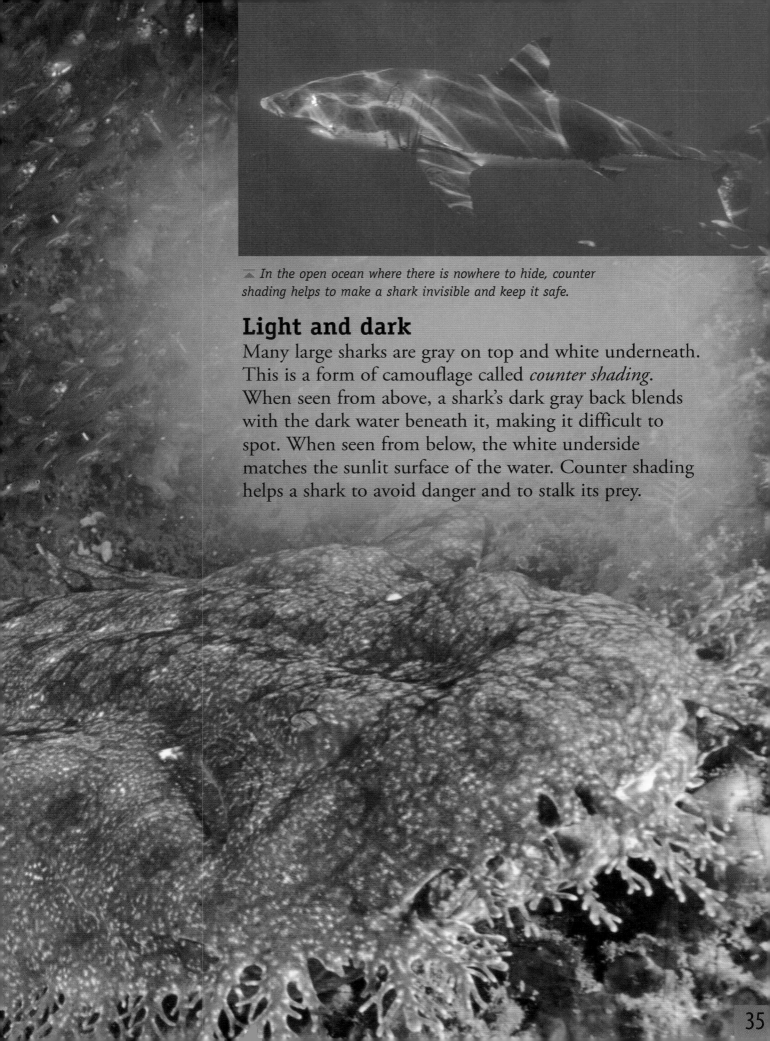

⌃ *In the open ocean where there is nowhere to hide, counter shading helps to make a shark invisible and keep it safe.*

Light and dark

Many large sharks are gray on top and white underneath. This is a form of camouflage called *counter shading*. When seen from above, a shark's dark gray back blends with the dark water beneath it, making it difficult to spot. When seen from below, the white underside matches the sunlit surface of the water. Counter shading helps a shark to avoid danger and to stalk its prey.

Growing Up

Sharks produce only a few young, but these are quite large and well developed and look like smaller versions of their parents. When they are born, baby sharks are left to look after themselves.

Egg cases

Baby sharks are called *pups*. Most sharks give birth to live young, but some lay eggs. Each egg is protected in a leathery case. The dogfish and swell shark lay egg cases with tendrils at each corner used to attach the egg to seaweed. Zebra sharks lay egg cases that stick to the seabed. Other sharks keep their eggs inside their bodies and then give birth to live pups.

This baby swell shark is just coming out of its egg case after growing inside for 9–12 months. Each egg case contains only one pup.

⏶ *The horn shark pushes its spiralled egg cases into crevices in the rocks to keep them safe. When the pup comes out, it will have to look after itself.*

Shark nurseries

A *nursery* is the name given to a place where sharks have their young or where young sharks gather. Sharks often lay their eggs near the shore where there are fewer large predators to attack the eggs and the newly hatched pups. Live-bearing sharks also come into shallow water to give birth. The pups are born with all their teeth. Their parents do not need to teach them how to hunt or survive—the young sharks are born knowing how to look after themselves.

Sharks and **Us**

We are both fascinated and terrified by sharks. Sharks are often seen as monsters to be hunted and slaughtered before they do the same to us.

Amazing creatures

The risk of death from being struck by lightning is 30 times greater than from an attack by a shark. Bees and snakes cause far more deaths each year than sharks. Out of the millions of people who enter the sea each year, as few as eight are killed by sharks. However, it is estimated that millions of sharks are killed by humans each year. Sharks are graceful and amazing creatures—they need our protection.

A huge fin sticking out of the water is used in movies to warn that there is a shark nearby and to scare the audience.

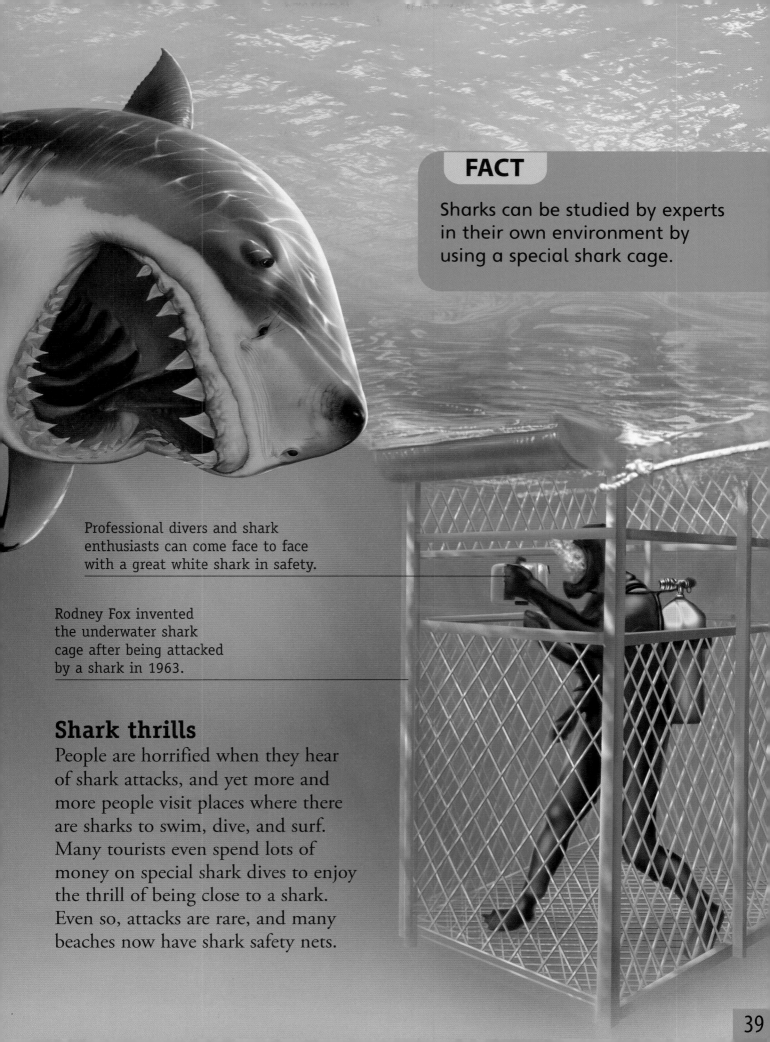

FACT

Sharks can be studied by experts in their own environment by using a special shark cage.

Professional divers and shark enthusiasts can come face to face with a great white shark in safety.

Rodney Fox invented the underwater shark cage after being attacked by a shark in 1963.

Shark thrills

People are horrified when they hear of shark attacks, and yet more and more people visit places where there are sharks to swim, dive, and surf. Many tourists even spend lots of money on special shark dives to enjoy the thrill of being close to a shark. Even so, attacks are rare, and many beaches now have shark safety nets.

Studying sharks

Long-term information about how and where sharks migrate, their growth rates, distribution, and other information is collected by tagging sharks. When a shark is tagged, scientists record its length, weight, sex, species, and details about where it was caught. Then, the shark is released. When the shark is caught again, it can be identified by a special number, and its location, size, and other details will be compared with the original information collected.

Some sharks have unique markings on their dorsal fins, which are used to identify them. This gives the experts information about the number of sharks in the area, when and where they migrate, and if they return.

Satellite tagging

Scientists also use near-real time satellite tags, which allow them to track the sharks daily. The tags record the location of the shark and collect information about the sea temperature and the depth to which the shark swims. Every time the shark comes to the surface, the tag sends a radio signal that is picked up by satellite and sent to land centers. The daily movements of the shark can then be plotted on a map. After a few months, the tags release themselves and float to the surface.

Light splotch

Two black spots

Nick on fin

Double nick

Understanding sharks

Shark research is providing new knowledge about how sharks live, and we are beginning to understand sharks a bit better. This will help us protect sharks, as many are endangered. Understanding sharks better will hopefully lead to increased safety for swimmers, too.

A baby hammerhead shark is weighed and measured before being tagged and released back into the ocean.

Endangered sharks

Many types of sharks are now endangered, including the great white shark, the blue shark, and the whale shark. This is because there are fewer traditional fish due to over-fishing, so more sharks are being caught to replace them. Sharks do not produce enough young to make up the number.

Just the fins

A shark's fins are worth more than the rest of the shark. The fins are hacked from the shark while it is still alive, and the shark is thrown back into the sea where it will die by drowning. The fins are used for shark fin soup.

▶| *The United Sates and the European Union have banned shark finning, but millions of sharks are still caught and killed every year for their fins.*

FACT

Research shows that about 270,000 sharks are killed each day for their meat or fins. This is sold in restaurants and supermarkets in some parts of the world, such as China and Indonesia.

▶ *Sharks' teeth are often made into jewelery. This is a necklace made from tiger shark teeth.*

Save the shark

Many countries have now agreed to stop shark fishing or put a limit on how many can be fished each year. In the UK, some supermarkets no longer sell shark meat. Conservation groups around the world are trying to teach people how important it is to stop our sharks from becoming extinct. Sharks are a reminder of life on Earth before humans developed, and they help to keep the seas clean by eating dead and diseased fish. It is our duty to look after them.

A conservation sign at a whale shark festival in the Philippines encourages young people to care for sharks.

Facts and Records

❦ Sharks play an important role in food chains of the ocean by preying on other predators, such as seals and octopuses. This keeps the numbers of these predators in balance with the rest of the food chain.

❦ A shark's body is rough because it is covered with skin teeth, which provide the shark with extra protection. In the past, shark skin was used as sandpaper.

❦ A whale shark might weigh 20 tons (18 tonnes), about the same as 500 children.

❦ Sharks "talk" to each other using body postures. A shark will hunch its back and raise its head when it feels threatened.

❦ Some sharks migrate long distances looking for food or a mate. The longest distance recorded for a whale shark is 8,078 mi. (13,000 km). A great white shark traveled 12,427 mi. (20,000 km) from Africa to Australia and back again.

A shark's streamlined shape helps it to slip through the water easily.

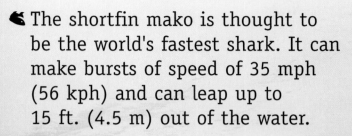

The shortfin mako is thought to be the world's fastest shark. It can make bursts of speed of 35 mph (56 kph) and can leap up to 15 ft. (4.5 m) out of the water.

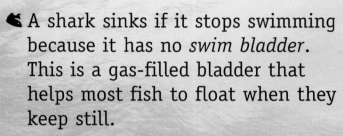

A shark sinks if it stops swimming because it has no *swim bladder*. This is a gas-filled bladder that helps most fish to float when they keep still.

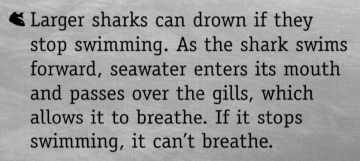

Larger sharks can drown if they stop swimming. As the shark swims forward, seawater enters its mouth and passes over the gills, which allows it to breathe. If it stops swimming, it can't breathe.

Bottom-living sharks have a hole called a *spiracle* in their heads.

spiracle

They use this to pump water and oxygen to their gills while resting on the sea bed.

Rays are related to sharks, and both have skeletons made of cartilage. In fact, rays are like flattened sharks that swim with winglike fins.

The manta ray is more than 21 ft. (6.5 m) long and is a harmless filter feeder.

45

Glossary

Barbels Fleshy, whiskerlike feelers near the mouth of some bottom-living sharks used to taste and feel.

Bioluminescence The production of light by living things such as deep-sea fish. Some of these animals have special organs that produce light by a chemical reaction; others have glowing bacteria that live on them.

Cartilage A light, flexible, supportive tissue.

Crustaceans A group of animals that have a hard external skeleton (exoskeleton), jointed legs, and a segmented body. Crabs and beetles are examples of crustaceans.

Dorsal fin The large fin on the back of a fish that helps to keep the animal upright. Some sharks have two dorsal fins.

Endangered When a species of animal or plant is in danger of becoming extinct, either through natural reasons or human activities.

Extinct An animal (or plant) that once lived but has now died out.

Live-bearing fish A fish that produces eggs but keeps them inside her body until they hatch, giving birth to live young.

Low-frequency sound Slow-moving soundwaves produce a deep or low-frequency sound. This is the opposite of fast-moving, high-frequency sounds, such as a dolphin's squeak.

Migrate When animals, such as some sharks, move from one area to another in search of food or a mate, or because of changes in temperature (for example, in winter or springtime).

Near-real time satellite tags These are attached to sharks to track their movements and habits. A satellite picks up the signal from the tag and sends it to the researcher's computer. Because of the time delay, this can only tell scientists where the shark was a few hours ago, which is why it is called near-real time.

Pectoral fins A pair of fins at the front of a shark behind the head. Sharks are front heavy, and these fins provide extra lift that helps the shark to swim straight.

Plankton Microscopic plants and tiny animals invisible to the human eye.

Predator An animal that hunts and feeds on other animals.

Prey Animals that are hunted and killed for food by predatory animals.

Satellite tag An electronic tag that can be attached to animals such as sharks. The tag gives off a signal that is picked up by a satellite.

Streamlined The shape of a shark that helps it to move easily through the water.

Subtropical An area of the world where the weather is warm and never gets really cold.

Temperate An area of the world where there are winter and summer seasons.

Tendrils Long, thin attachments at the corners of some shark egg cases.

SHARK SIZE BY LENGTH

Spined pygmy shark
5 in. (20 cm)

Cookie cutter shark
19 in. (50 cm)

Port Jackson shark
4.5 ft. (1.4 m)

Nurse shark
9 ft. (3 m)

Tasselled wobbegong shark
9–13 ft. (3–4 m)

Sand tiger shark
10 ft. (3.2 m)

Bull shark
11 ft. (3.3 m)

Lemon shark
11 ft. (3.4 m)

Blue shark
11 ft. (3.5 m)

Porbeagle shark
12 ft. (3.7 m)

Common thresher shark
16–19 ft. (5–6 m)

Tiger shark
18 ft. (5.5 m)

Great hammerhead shark
19 ft. (6 m)

Great white shark
21 ft. (6.6 m)

Basking shark
39 ft. (11 m)

Whale shark
40 ft. (12 m)

Index